THE I HATE WENDY CLUB

Story, Lessons, and Activities on Relational Aggression
Grades 2–5

WRITTEN BY
Debra Wosnik

ILLUSTRATED BY
Jeffrey Zwartjes

DEDICATION

To my sister Wendy, a remarkable woman!
I don't know what my life would be like without her.
I am glad to include her in everything.

THE I HATE WENDY CLUB

10-DIGIT ISBN: 1-57543-153-X
13-DIGIT ISBN: 978-1-57543-153-6

Published by mar*co products, inc.
1443 Old York Road
Warminster, PA 18974
1-800-448-2197
www.marcoproducts.com

PRINTED IN THE U.S.A.

Contents

Introduction

This program includes an original story and series of lessons and supplementary activities that teach and reinforce the concept of *relational aggression.* The story is about a little girl and her sisters, who start a club they won't allow her to join. When the girls' mother finds out about the club, she explains *relational aggression* to her older daughters. The girls decide that including everyone is more fun than leaving anyone out. They learn to understand what it feels like to be excluded.

Follow-up lessons are included for use when presenting the story (pages 9-32). The follow-up lessons include:

- ***The I Hate Wendy Club:*** This lesson teaches children to write rules for a club that includes everyone. It corresponds to the story and gives the students an opportunity to brainstorm ways to include others and create colorful posters that invite everyone to join their club.

- ***Welcome To Our School:*** This lesson reminds me of the neighborhood Welcome Wagon®. Students fill bags with useful items for students new to the school. The welcoming students participate in every aspect of the activity, from planning which items to include to decorating and delivering the bags. Children love to help newcomers, and this lesson reinforces the importance of including others and making a fresh start by not gossiping.

- ***Draw You In To Make 10:*** This lesson uses math manipulatives to count out the factors of 10. The T-shirts illustrate how each friend brings something different to a group. Because each student draws a number on the blank T-shirt to make all the numbers on all three shirts add up to 10, this lesson is a great math review. It also showcases individual talents.

- ***You Be The Judge:*** Using big numbered cards like Olympic judges use to rate athletes' performances, each student votes for the best answer to each question about *relational aggression.* After the leader reads the description of each problem, each student holds up the card whose number corresponds to the answer he/she would choose. The fact that there are several right answers to each question encourages discussion of this important topic.

- ***The Yacht Club:*** Homemade walnut-shell boats are an essential part of this fun lesson. A student earns a turn to race one of the little boats when the club president calls that student's number or color. This activity provides an important learning experience on *exclusion.* It also gives the students an opportunity to talk about feelings and make changes in the structure of the club.

An optional pre-test and a post-test may be used to evaluate the lessons' effectiveness.

The pre-test is on page 6. The answers are: 1–4; 2–6; 3–2; 4–3; 5–7; 6–5; 7–8; 8–1; 9-10; 10–9.

The post-test is found on page 7. The answers are:

purposely
exclude
invitation
gossip
relationship
aggression
include
president
bylaw
threaten

This series of lessons helps students recognize any aspects of their own behavior that could be considered *relational aggression.* It also teaches students to recognize relational aggression in others and develop the skills to do something to deflect or prevent the behavior.

Pre-Test

Name ____

Directions: Read the list of words below. Then read the sentences that follow them and find the one that gives each word's meaning. Write the number of the sentence that gives the meaning of a word on the blank line following the word.

1. gossip ________
2. relationship ________
3. aggression ________
4. president ________
5. bylaw ________
6. include ________
7. exclude ________
8. invitation ________
9. threaten ________
10. purposely ________

1. This is a note or message used to ask someone to do something or go somewhere.
2. This means attack, assault, or hostile behavior.
3. This is the chief officer of a club.
4. This means to repeat something someone has told you or to talk about someone's private business.
5. This means to let in or contain.
6. This means a feeling that exists between people.
7. This is a rule or basic law for a club.
8. This means to shut out or reject.
9. This means to show or say that you intend to do something.
10. This is to say or show that you are going to do something mean.

Post-Test

Name ________________________________

Directions: Read each of the following sentences. Read the words that follow the sentences. On each blank line, write the word that completes the sentence correctly.

1. If I mean to hurt someone, I hurt that person on purpose or ________________ .
2. If I don't let my friend join my club, I ________________ her.
3. A courteous request to go somewhere or do something is an ________________ .
4. If a friend repeats something I told her, that is ________________ .
5. If someone has been my friend for a long time, we have a ________________ .
6. Throwing a chair is an act of ________________ .
7. If I let my friend play, I ________________ her in the game.
8. If I am the leader of a club, I am called the ________________ .
9. A rule for a club is called a ________________ .
10. If I ________________ someone, I let him/her know that I want to hurt him/her in some way.

gossip	**relationship**	**aggression**	**president**
bylaw	**include**	**invitation**	**exclude**
threaten	**purposely**		

THE
I HATE WENDY
CLUB
PRESIDENT : CHER
VICE PRESIDENT : DEBRA
-NO ONE NAMED WENDY
ALLOWED!!!!!!!!

The I Hate Wendy Club

BALL ROOM

I don't remember why we started **The I Hate Wendy Club**. Maybe it was because Wendy lifted my friend Gerald over the door of the room where balls were stored and all the balls fell on his head.

Or because of the time she unscrewed the bolts under the cafeteria tables and all the lunch trays started to slide down toward my friends and me.

It could have been because of the day she put the flattened dead frog in her top drawer so we wouldn't borrow her clothes.

Or the day she accidentally set her bug collection free in our bedroom.

For some reason or other, **The I Hate Wendy Club** was born one day. My older sister Cher and I made a handwritten poster on paper and taped it to our bedroom door. It announced that we had formed **The I Hate Wendy Club**.

We had a few rules and bylaws. But the main rule was: **You could not be our little sister Wendy and be a member of our club.**

I don't remember how the club began, but I remember that it ended the minute Mom walked past our bedroom door and read the poster.

I remember what Mom told us that day. "When you leave someone out," she said, "you hurt her feelings. And hurt feelings are just as painful as a hurt body." This was news to me. I had been in trouble before for hitting my sisters, but never for leaving them out.

Mom explained how it feels to be **excluded**. That was a big word, but I remember the feeling...

Like when everyone in your class gets an invitation to a birthday party and you don't. It feels sad.

Or when girls you thought were your friends don't want to sit with you at lunch.

Or when your friends go to a parade and don't ask you to go with them. You feel a pain inside your chest.

The more you like the friends, the worse you feel when they exclude you.

When someone is friendly some of the time and cruel to the same people at other times, this is called **relational aggression**.

If you're older and have more power than the other person, relational aggression is like being a bully who doesn't hit or make threats.

When you care about someone, you have a relationship with that person. My sisters and my friends have relationships with me. We share fun times together.

We all have relationships with our friends. Purposely excluding them or gossiping about them is relational aggression. When Cher and I realized what we were doing, we decided we didn't want to make our little sister feel sad.

Cher and I invited Wendy to join our club. The three of us had a fun afternoon.

We decided to change the name of the club. Since that time, our club has had many meetings. Wendy was even club president for a while. And as the years went by, our club added two more members: Mary Anne and Holly (our littlest sisters).

We found out that it is more fun to include everyone than to exclude anyone. Each person brings something special to the group. Wendy is funny. She makes us all laugh. She always has good ideas about games to play. She is smart and interesting. She likes to sing and play the guitar.

If we had left her out, we would have missed out. So, if people bug you...

It's better to work everything out than to leave anyone out!
!

LESSONS

LESSON 1

The I Hate Wendy Club

Goals:

- To introduce the concept of *relational aggression* and help students understand that hurting feelings harms friendships
- To help students understand that excluding friends causes hard feelings
- To help students recognize that including everyone adds fun to any group
- To encourage students to look for the good qualities in friends and refrain from gossip

Materials Needed:

For the leader:
- ☐ Copy of *The I Hate Wendy Club* poster (page 37)
- ☐ Whiteboard and marker or chalkboard and chalk

For each student or group:
- ☐ Copy of *The I Hate Wendy Club* poster (pages 37)
- ☐ Paper
- ☐ Pencil
- ☐ Crayons

Lesson Preparation:

Draw the entire *I Hate Wendy Club* poster (page 37) on the board. Reproduce a copy of the poster (page 37) for each student group or student.

Lesson:

Introduce the lesson by saying:

> *Everyone loves to belong to a club. When I was small, I belonged to* ______ ________ (Girl Scouts, Brownies, Big Brothers, etc.). *We did fun things. We helped people. One time, we* (SOMETHING FUN YOU DID AS A CHILD AS A MEMBER OF A CLUB).

Ask the students the following questions:

> *What clubs do you know about?*
>
> *What kind of activities do members of those clubs enjoy?*

Then say:

> *I'm going to read a true story about two sisters who started their own club. They decided which one of them would be club president. They decided who could be in the club and who would be left out. Listen carefully to the story and decide if this is the kind of club you would like to join.*

Read *The I Hate Wendy Club* (pages 9-32).

When you have finished reading the story, ask the following questions:

> *Why were the girls mad at their little sister*? (She threw a friend over the door of the room where balls were stored. She unscrewed the legs of a table and embarrassed her sister. She put bugs and a dead frog in the girls' bedroom.)
>
> *Did Wendy's sisters have good reasons to be angry with her?* (Yes.)
>
> *How did Wendy's older sisters feel?* (They may have felt embarrassed, frustrated, scared, worried, and any other appropriate feeling.)
>
> *How do you think Wendy felt about being left out?* (She may have felt sad, disappointed, unloved, and any other appropriate feeling.)
>
> *What special things about Wendy did her sisters miss when they kept her out of the club*? (They missed laughing at her funny ways, her good ideas, and her singing and playing the guitar.)
>
> *Is it ever OK to leave someone out?* (Yes, it is OK to leave someone out when the person tries to exert peer pressure to have you do something that is violent or against your values.)
>
> *Would you like to be a member of The I Hate Wendy Club?* (No.) *Why not?* (Accept all appropriate answers.)

Conclusion:

Tell the students:

> *The next activity has to do with the story you just heard. You may decide if you want to work alone or with other students in our class, as part of a group.*

Have the students select which way they would like to work. Everyone must work individually or everyone must work in groups.

If the students decide they want to work in groups, remind them that everyone who wants to be part of a group is welcome to join it. (The result of this lesson should be that the students include everyone in the group.) After the groups are formed, compliment the students for using inviting words and including everyone who wanted to join a group.

If the students decide they will work alone, this becomes a class activity.

Distribute *The I Hate Wendy Club* poster and a piece of paper to each group of students if the students are working in groups. If the students are working individually, distribute *The I Hate Wendy Club* poster and a piece of paper to each student. Make sure all the students have pencils and crayons.

Continue the lesson by telling the students that the club in the story was renamed after Wendy's sisters decided to include her. Have the students brainstorm new names for the club and design posters that reflect *inclusion.* Examples of titles for posters could be: *We Love Everyone Club* or *No Child Left Out Club*. Tell the students to write club bylaws on their posters.

Display the poster(s) on a bulletin board for the week as reminders to include every classmate in every activity. If possible, check in with the students after each recess to make sure the rules of inclusion are being followed on the playground as well as in the classroom.

THE
I HATE WENDY
CLUB
PRESIDENT: CHER
VICE PRESIDENT: DEBRA
-NO ONE NAMED WENDY
ALLOWED!!!!

LESSON 2

Welcome To Our School

Goals:

- To help new students feel welcome
- To encourage students to help someone who needs a friend
- To learn empathy for students in a new situation
- To give people a fresh start and refrain from gossip

Materials Needed:

For the leader:
- ☐ A map of the school (optional)
- ☐ Pencils, magnets, granola bars, and other items to place in lunch bags

For each student:
- ☐ Piece of unlined paper
- ☐ White lunch bag
- ☐ Crayons or markers
- ☐ Pencil

Lesson Preparation:

Order lunch bags from the cafeteria manager or school-supply warehouse. Walk around the school to see which areas may need to be described to a new student. Gather any other necessary materials.

Lesson:

Introduce the lesson by saying:

> *When we read the story of the girls not letting their sister join their club, we realize that being excluded hurts people. How many of you were new to our school this year? How did you feel the first day you came to this school? Did you feel left out? New students often feel left out because other students already have their groups of friends. Sometimes it takes a while for a student to make*

good friends in a new school. Even if you already have lots of friends, it's exciting to get to know new boys and girls and include them in your activities. This project can help our new friends feel at home in our school. We're going to make Welcome To (NAME OF SCHOOL) School Bags. *What things can we include in these bags that would be helpful for our new friends?*

Listen to all the students' suggestions. Then continue:

I think a new student might need a map to figure out how to get around. We might want to show where to find the restrooms, lunchroom, library, etc.

Give each student a piece of unlined paper and a white lunch bag. Have each student take out crayons and a pencil. On the unlined paper, the students should draw a map of the school, labeling the areas mentioned. (If you have a map of the school, allow the students to refer to it if they need help drawing their maps.) Then have each student decorate a white lunch bag with a drawing (school mascot, flag, playground, etc.). Encourage the students to suggest the messages and pictures they can use to decorate the bags. (*Welcome to our school. We are glad you are a Bluff Ridge Bison,* etc.)

Have the students brainstorm ideas for other things to put in the bags. (A granola bar with a typed message such as: *We want our new friends to know…* or *We are allowed to eat only in the lunchroom;* laminated refrigerator magnets with school rules or calendars of events; and/or flash cards made from old yearbooks and labeled with the names of the staff members on the back and their photos on the front: Mrs. Welch is our librarian. This is what she looks like. If some suggestions require items the students can't make themselves, explain that you will purchase these items outside class and put them in the bags.

When the students have finished decorating the bags and putting their maps and other articles into them, say:

Now we have bags for 30 (or whatever number of students are in the class/group) students who are new to our school during the year. Can we use them for children who are not in our grade? Yes, we welcome them all!

Conclusion:

Conclude the lesson by saying:

Everybody gets a fresh start when someone new comes to our school. We should never gossip about anyone or share negative information. We want each of our new friends to find out for him/herself which students would make good friends.

LESSON 3

Draw You In To Make 10

Goals:

- To help students understand that we all need each other
- To help students understand that each friend can bring positive attributes to a group
- To help students review the addition factors of 10

Materials Needed:

For the leader:
None

For each student:
- ☐ *Friends* (page 42)
- ☐ 10 math manipulatives of the same object (plastic objects, marshmallows, etc.)
- ☐ Cup or bag
- ☐ Pencil
- ☐ Crayons

Lesson Preparation:

Reproduce a copy of *Friends* for each student. Count out 10 objects and put them into a cup or bag.

Lesson:

Give each student a copy of *Friends* and a cup containing 10 manipulatives. Make sure each student has a pencil and crayons. Then introduce the activity by saying:

> *I will explain this activity to you, but I need your help. The objects on your desk are to be used later. Please keep them in the cup/bag while we are talking about today's math exercise. Look at your worksheet. As you can see, children wearing T-shirts are pictured on this page. There is a number on each T-shirt. Let's see if we can make the numbers on the T-shirts worn by a group of friends add up to 10. The first friend is wearing a shirt that has the number 2. The friend next to her is wearing the number 4. Next to the two friends, draw a friend who*

is wearing the T-shirt. On the new friend's shirt, draw the number that would make this group's numbers add up to 10. Yes, the number would have to be a 4. Now take one object from your cup for each number on the three shirts. Check to see if you were right. Put your manipulatives back into the cup and continue with the next problem on the page.

The numbers in parentheses are the numbers the students should have written on the T-shirts.

2+4 (4)
1+9 (0)
8+1 (1)
6+2 (2)
7+1 (2)
6+1 (3)

Continue the lesson by saying:

Now turn your paper over. On the back, draw some friends wearing T-shirts. On each shirt, write a word that is a good quality for a friend to have. For example, you could write: Kindness, Sportsmanship, Honesty.

Conclusion:

Conclude the lesson by saying:

We all want to have lots of friends. We need friends who are fast runners in case we have an emergency. We need friends who are good readers to help us sound out words. We need friends who are tall to reach things up high. We should never exclude a friend from our group. We all need all of our friends, so we can share our talents and friendship.

F
R
I
E
N
D
S

2
4

6
2

1
9

7
1

8
1

6
1

LESSON 4

You Be The Judge

Goals:

- To help students discover several ways to handle being excluded
- To help students develop strategies to use with friends
- To help students address gossiping

Materials Needed:

For the leader:
☐ Black marker

For each student:
☐ 4 pieces of tagboard numbered 1, 2, 3, and 4
☐ Plastic binder (optional)

Lesson Preparation:

Write the numbers *1, 2, 3,* and *4* on the tagboard in very large print. Write one number on each piece of tagboard. Make a set of numbers for each participating student.

Lesson:

Distribute four pieces of tagboard to each student. Have the students lay the pieces of tagboard out on their desks or bind them so that as you read each problem, they can flip to the number they choose.

Introduce the lesson by saying:

> *Look inside your desks and find your crayons. Look at the box and find the word* non-toxic. *What does that word mean? Right. It means* it can't hurt you. *What do you think* toxic *would mean? Oh, yes, something that is toxic could hurt you. Can friends sometimes hurt you?*

Everyone has problems with friends sometimes. Your friend may be having a bad day. Or he or she may be a toxic friend, a friend who can hurt you. Whether your friend is having a bad day or is toxic, you'll be faced with situations that you must handle. In most cases, you'll have to decide very quickly how to handle the situation.

I'm going to read some scenarios about friends. I will read the description of each problem. Then I'll read four ways to handle it. You will be like the judges at the Olympic Games and hold up the number of the suggestion that you think best solves the problem. For some problems, more than one suggestion may be a good answer. You should hold up the number that is the same as the number of the answer you think is best. We will discuss each answer and why it might or might not be helpful.

We'll start by setting the rules. Place the numbered pieces of tagboard on the right-hand corner of your desk and fold your hands in your lap. As I read each problem, take a minute to think about your objective.

- *What do you want to happen?*
- *Do you want to get revenge or do you want to keep a friend?*
- *Your answer will reflect your objective. This is not a race. Don't worry about whether you are the first one to hold up the card that shows what answer you think is best. Think carefully about the best way to solve the problem. After you have decided which answer you think is best, hold up the piece of tagboard with the number that is the best answer for you.*

In almost every class, someone picks the silly answer and tries to get attention by holding up the wrong number. We will ignore anyone in this class who does that, and I will speak to that student privately after class. In order to make this activity fun for everyone, try your best to give good answers. I'll know you're ready to play when everyone's hands are folded in his or her lap. (This instruction discourages students from playing with the numbered sheets of tagboard while you read the situation descriptions to them.)

Read the description of the first situation:

Your friend e-mails that everyone is talking about you.

Would you …

1. *e-mail back with some gossip you heard?*
2. *tell your friend you don't want to be told things like that?*

3. *talk with an adult about what you should do?*
4. *ignore the e-mail and go about your day?*

Allow time for the students to think, choose a response, and hold up the appropriate card. Then continue the activity by reading the remaining scenario descriptions:

Your close friend invites someone else to the movies but doesn't invite you.

Would you …

1. *storm off and say that you're through being that person's friend?*
2. *let it go and see whom your friend invites next time?*
3. *invite your friend and the other person to go with you to a movie next week?*
4. *spread rumors about your friend's new friend?*

Your friend is nice to you one day and mean the next day. You never know what to expect.

Would you …

1. *send your friend an "I" Message telling him/her how you feel when he/she is mean to you?*
2. *have all of your friends confront the person who is behaving this way?*
3. *watch how your friend acts with others to see if he/she treats everyone the same way?*
4. *send your friend a mean note?*

Someone you really like does not like your other friends.

Would you …

1. *divide your time between your new friend and your other friends?*
2. *spread lies over the Internet about your old friends so they will leave you alone?*
3. *tell your new friend all the good things about your other friends?*
4. *ask an adult for advice?*

Some kids on the playground start a club and say you can't join it.

Would you …

1. *ignore them and start your own club?*
2. *beg and whine to be allowed to join the club?*

3. *give the kids who started the club the cookies from your lunch?*
4 *start rumors about the club so nobody wants to join?*

Your best friend is really friendly with a new student in school.

Would you …

1. *start rumors about the new student so nobody will play with him/her?*
2. *start playing with someone else?*
3. *wait and see what happens?*
4. *tell your best friend that you're worried about your friendship?*

Your friend pressures you to steal something from a store.

Would you …

1. *tell your friend you would never do that?*
2. *start looking for a new friend?*
3. *explain your values to your friend?*
4. *tell your friend that you want only friends who are honest?*

Your best friend is starting to hit you in a playful way. But those punches really hurt!

Would you …

1. *hit your friend back harder than he/she hit you?*
2. *talk privately with your friend about the problem?*
3. *tell other people that you don't like what your friend is doing?*
4. *tell your friend that you'll tell an adult If he/she doesn't stop hitting you?*

Your neighborhood friend is bullying you at school but is friendly at home.

Would you …

1. *point this out to your friend in a calm way?*
2. *not talk with this friend at school?*
3. *ask the guidance counselor to speak with your friend about his/her behavior?*
4. *tell your friend to stop bullying you?*

Gina tells you a rumor about your best friend.

Would you …

1. *immediately tell your best friend what Gina said about her?*
2. *stick up for your best friend by telling Gina to stop spreading the rumor?*
3. *start rumors about Gina?*
4. *tell Gina her outfit looks dumb?*

Bill tells you something bad about Tim.

Would you …

1. *tell Bill another bad thing you know about Tim?*
2. *tell Bill you can't talk about it because Tim isn't there?*
3. *call your other friends over to hear the gossip?*
4. *drop Tim as your friend because of the gossip?*

Conclusion:

Collect the tagboard. Then conclude the lesson by saying:

> *Deciding what to do can be difficult. You may think of several good ways to handle a situation and some ways that are not so good. The best thing to do is to think about your objective. Is your objective to keep a good friend? Is your objective to get revenge? Ask yourself questions and take your time. It's always great to have an adult help you decide.*

LESSON 5

The Yacht Club

Goals:

- To help students understand the meaning of *exclusion*
- To help students identify feelings resulting from being excluded
- To assist students in developing teamwork skills

Materials Needed:

For the leader:

- ☐ Large, shallow pan of water
- ☐ Walnut halves (one for each student, one for the leader)
- ☐ Table knife
- ☐ Modeling dough or clay
- ☐ Toothpicks
- ☐ White paper, copy weight

For each student:

- ☐ One walnut half
- ☐ About 1 tablespoon of modeling dough or clay
- ☐ One toothpick
- ☐ Crayons or markers
- ☐ Scissors
- ☐ White paper (1 sheet)

Lesson Preparation:

The best way to cut a walnut exactly in half is to squeeze the nut until it breaks open in the natural place, then slide a table knife under the shell and pry the nut open. Obtain enough walnuts for every student in the class to have a walnut half. Gather the other necessary materials.

Lesson:

Distribute one-half walnut shell, a toothpick, a piece of white paper, scissors, and about a tablespoon of modeling dough or clay to each student. Make sure each student has crayons or markers.

Introduce the lesson by saying:

> *We are going to make little sailboats. The boats are easy to make. Just follow along as you listen to my directions.* (Demonstrate making a walnut sailboat as you give the directions.) *Just fill the walnut with the clay. Cut a sail out of white paper. I want you to decorate the sail, using any two colors you choose and one number. Then insert the toothpick through the sail. Push the toothpick into the clay. Now put away your crayons and markers.*

When the students have completed their sailboats, walk around the room and silently choose a number found on one or two boats. Choose one of the colors the students used on their sails. Then continue the lesson by saying:

> *I want to tell you about my yacht club. I am the club president. I make the rules. A boat in my club may only have the number (NUMBER CHOSEN) on its sail. If you have the number (NUMBER CHOSEN) on your sail, you may race your boat in my yacht club.*

Have the students whose boats have that number place the boats in the pan of water. When you say, "Go!" each child should blow on his/her sail, racing the sailboats to the other side of the pan.

After the children with the chosen number finish their race, ask the other students in the class:

> *Wasn't that fun?*
>
> *Did you all have fun doing* that? (The common answer will be "No. It wasn't fun for me because I didn't get to play.")
>
> *How did you feel?* (Answers could include *left out, bored, disappointed,* etc.)
>
> *Can I change the bylaws of my club?* (Yes.)

Then say:

> *You're right. I can change my club's bylaws and that's exactly what I'm going to do. Instead of those with the (NUMBER CHOSEN) on their sail being able to race, those whose sails include the color (COLOR CHOSEN) may race.*

After the children whose sails include the chosen color finish their race, ask the other students in the class:

> *Was that more fun?* (No. It wasn't fun, because not everyone got a chance to play.)
>
> *OK, what could we do to include everyone? How could we all race at the same time?* (Let the children come up with ideas that will let everyone play.)

Conclusion:

Conclude the lesson by saying:

> *Some people belong to clubs or groups or gangs. The people who belong to a particular group make up the rules for their group. It's a good idea to let everyone decide what the rules should be. A team works best when it uses everyone's ideas. It's important for everyone not to talk at once, but it's also important to listen to everyone's ideas.*
>
> *As a member of a club or group, what could you do if the leader suggested something that would hurt others?* (Speak up, like bystanders should do when a bully threatens someone.)
>
> *Clubs need rules so that things can be orderly. A club whose rules exclude people because of their race, religion, skin color, how much money they have, etc. is not a fun club. Leaders of groups sometimes use things like brand-name clothes or skin color to bully others, leave them out, or put them down. That is* relational aggression. *Deciding who can be in a group based on things like these causes people to react in unfriendly ways. If you're a member of a group like this, you can speak up.*

SUPPLEMENTARY ACTIVITIES

SUPPLEMENTARY ACTIVITY INSTRUCTIONS

FRIENDLY FOOD (pages 58-59)
The purpose of this activity is to show that including more people can make everyone happier. To complete this activity, each student will need the activity sheets, crayons, scissors, and a gluestick. Distribute the activity sheet and have the students color their favorite foods. Have them cut out the foods and paste them in the melting pot. When reviewing the activity sheets with the class, discuss how various foods were brought to America. If we had excluded people from Italy, we wouldn't have pizza. If we had excluded people from Germany, we wouldn't be eating hot dogs. Everyone brings something special to a group.

INCLUDE/EXCLUDE (page 60)
The purpose of this activity is to help students associate feelings with being included or excluded from something. To complete this activity, each student will need a copy of the activity sheet and a pencil. Have the students brainstorm, with the leader, about how they might feel if they were included in an activity. Write their suggestions on the board. Then have them describe how they might feel if they were excluded. Write their suggestions on the board. Distribute the activity sheet to each student. Make sure each student has a pencil. Students in lower grades will perform this activity as a class/group. Older students will write the appropriate feelings in the circles labeled *exclude* and *include.* Tell the students to write each of the words listed next to the circles inside the proper circle. Then they may add to their circles the words written on the board.

To complete the second half of this page, students will write *I* next to statements of inclusion and *E* next to statements that exclude. Tell the students to read each sentence and decide if that statement would *include* friends or *exclude* them from play. Answers: 1–I; 2–E; 3–I; 4–E; 5–E; 6–E; 7–I; 8–E; 9–E; 10–I; 11–I.

THE GOSSIP GUARANTEE (page 61)
The purpose of this activity is to help students understand what *gossip* is and why it's harmful. To complete this activity, each student will need a copy of the activity sheet and a pencil. Have each student write a caption for each cartoon panel, changing the sentence by one word as each character whispers something to the next character. The last panel shows that the meaning of the original sentence has completely changed. Have a few students tell the class what captions they wrote. Discuss how words repeated by different people get changed by accident or on purpose. Assure the students that words and meanings change each time something is repeated. Emphasize that gossip is a waste of time. *Gossip* is definitely *relational aggression*. It causes hurt feelings and can exclude people. People who know you gossip will think they can't trust you. Gossip doesn't build relationships. It tears them down.

SNOWFLAKES (page 62)

The purpose of this activity is to reinforce the concept of *differences.* People are all different. When we accept and enjoy our differences, relational aggression diminishes. For this activity, each student will need a copy of the activity sheet, a pencil, paper, and scissors. Tell the students to cut out the snowflake on the activity sheet, then draw another snowflake on the paper and cut it out. As each student places his/her unique snowflake on the bulletin board, beauty is added to the classroom.

INVISIBLE INK CLUB (page 63)

The purpose of this activity is to address the existence of secret clubs. This activity helps students realize that adults can be a great help in making decisions about *inclusion.* The students cannot perform this activity without an adult. Each student will need a copy of the activity sheet, a lemon, a container, and a cotton swab or paintbrush. Cut each lemon in half before beginning the activity. Have the students squeeze each piece of lemon into a small container, then use a cotton swab/paintbrush to write their clubs' names on the activity sheet. After the message dries, the adult can use a warm iron to reveal the secret. When everyone's club's name has been revealed, talk with the students about why the adult, not a student, used the iron. Ask the students if there are some things children cannot or should not do without the help of an adult. Explain that keeping secrets from Mom and Dad about a surprise party is good, but it isn't always a good idea to do things others ask us to do in a secret way. Remind the students to always ask themselves if Mom, Dad, or their teacher would approve. Advise them to rely on the adults in their lives to help them make good choices.

PARADE (page 64)

The purpose of this activity is to reinforce the idea of *the more, the merrier*. Each student will need a copy of the activity sheet, crayons, and a pencil. Have the students color the band instruments on the activity sheet, then draw a line from the band member to the missing instrument. Just as a complete band produces a fuller sound, outside recess can be more fun if lots of people are included in the games.

EXCLUDING/INCLUDING VOWELS (page 65)

The purpose of this activity is to help students understand the importance of *vowels* in each word. Each student needs a copy of the activity sheet and a pencil. Tell the students that missing letters make words hard to read. When we leave friends out, we miss out on the chance to learn to understand lots of people. For younger students, write the following words on the board: *gossip, relationship, aggression, president, bylaws, include, exclude, invitation, threaten, purposely.* The students should refer to these words when completing the activity sheet. Older students can complete the activity sheet without having the words written on the board. Conclude the activity by telling the students that just as vowels are important parts of words, other people are important parts of our lives. They add interest and help us form our personalities.

COMPARE AND CONTRAST LETTER (page 66)

The purpose of this activity is to give the students an opportunity to practice letter-writing skills while explaining their feelings to a friend. Each student needs a copy of the activity sheet and a pencil. When someone is unkind to us, it can be hard to put our feelings into words. This activity uses an "I" Message to tell a friend that something he/she is doing is causing problems with the friendship. The *compare and contrast* part of the letter allows the writer to compliment the friend for what he/she feels is right with the friendship. This is a great way to combine a Language Arts lesson with a lesson on friendship.

INVITATIONS (pages 67-69)

The purpose of this activity is to give students a forum, through an art activity, to invite friends to play. Students often complain that they don't have any friends when the problem is that they don't know how to initiate play activities. Each student needs a copy of one of the activity sheets, a pencil, and crayons. Students should write the text of the invitation, color the invitation, and fold it in half, then in half again. For examples of what to write, the teacher cold suggest: *Meet me at the tetherball pole at recess for a fun game! Meet me at the blacktop at recess. Bring a jump rope*. Remind the students that these invitations are only for recess. A student who finishes early may create an original invitation on a blank sheet of paper. (Wallpaper sample books, construction paper, or scrapbook paper could also be used for the original invitations.)

WHAT IS WENDY'S TALENT? (page 70)

The purpose of this activity is to practice putting numbers in the correct sequence. Each student needs a copy of the activity sheet, a pencil, and crayons. When the dots are all connected, Wendy's talent appears (a guitar). The students may color the page after connecting the dots.

GET THE BUGS INTO THE JAR (page 71)

The purpose of this activity is to try to get the bugs back into the jar by tracing the lines that lead from each bug to the jar. Each student will need a copy of the activity sheet and a pencil. The discussion after this activity should include the topic of *mistakes*. Suggested questions are*: Did some of you start to follow a line in the wrong direction? If you see yourself as someone who has been unfriendly or has made some mistakes, is it OK to start in a new direction?* The answer to this last question is, "Yes, nobody is perfect. We all make mistakes with our relationships. It is important to keep trying."

FIND WENDY'S HIDDEN TALENTS (page 72)

The purpose of this activity is to remind students to look for the good in their friends. Each student will need a copy of the activity sheet and crayons. This activity uses hidden pictures. Tell the students to look closely to find the hidden pictures. Reinforce the activity by telling the students that just as they looked carefully at the activity sheet and discovered hidden pictures, they will discover hidden talents if they look closely at their friends. Remind the students that it's easy to see friends' faults. Encourage them to try this week to see the good things about their friends and compliment them for those qualities.

EXs AND INs (page 73)

The purpose of this activity is to encourage the students to use the dictionary to find words that begin with *ex* or *in.* The word a student finds must be able to stand alone without the *in* or *ex* prefix. Each student will need a copy of the activity sheet and a pencil. Give the students a set amount of time (20 minutes for upper grades) and have them list, in two columns, all the words they find. Have the student with the longest list come to the front of the classroom and read his/her list to the rest of the class. The students will check off each word on their own lists that matches a word being read. After the student who found the most words has finished reading his/her list, students who found other words will tell the class what words they found. This activity demonstrates how including everyone benefits us all. In this case, the whole class wins. Using everyone's list makes everyone else's list longer. In this activity, nobody loses. A possible homework assignment could be to add to the list with help from parents and other adults.

BUG FRIENDS (page 74)

The purpose of this activity is to find which bugs are exactly alike. Each student needs a copy of the activity sheet and a pencil. When everyone has completed the activity sheet, initiate a discussion of such points as: *Do we have to have friends who are just like us? Could they be older? Younger? Taller? Shorter? Can they look different? Have different kinds of hair? Do our friends have to like to play every game we like? Have the same color skin? Like to read the kind of books we like? Be good at sports? Be not so good at sports? How do we choose our friends?*

MY SECRET CLUB MESSAGE (page 75)

The purpose of this activity is for the students to get as many friends as they can to write letters in secret code. Reproduce the code and give a copy to each student. Then the students will use their own pencils and paper to write letters to their friends. This should start as a class activity, especially with students in lower grades. Students may write their letters in code and exchange them with classmates. If you have a classroom postal system, this activity would work well. If you don't have a classroom postal system, make sure the students understand the appropriate time to write and send these notes. This activity is more fun when everyone knows the secret, because there are more people to write. Having pen pals in another classroom or grade level would extend the activity to even more participants. Gifted students may want to devise a unique and different code. Remind them to share that code with everyone in the class.

HOW MANY WORDS CAN YOU MAKE? (page 76)

The purpose of this activity is to see how many small words students can form from the letters in RELATIONAL AGGRESSION. Each student will need a copy of the activity sheet and a pencil. This activity is designed to reinforce the students' understanding of the term *relational aggression.* Remind them that this behavior is a form of bullying by someone they know. The bully could even be a sometime-friend of the student he/she is bullying. When everyone has finished finding words, have the student with the longest list read his/her words to the class. The students should check off any words on their own lists that are the same as the ones being read. When the first student has finished reading his/her list of words, other students may continue the activity until every student has checked every word on his/her list.

MAKE A CASE FOR YOUR FRIEND (page 77)

The purpose of this activity is to help students learn to see friends objectively. No friend is perfect, but students may need to find new friends if their friends are harming them in any way. Each student needs a copy of the activity sheet and a pencil. The cases allow students to list what they like about a friend and the friend's actions that upset them. Reviewing this list with a parent or counselor may help the student decide if this friendship is a good one. This activity can also be the springboard for the student to deliver some "I" Messages to the friend. Adults may ask questions about behavior's cause and effect to see if each friend is partly responsible for the problems in the friendship.

COLORING PAGES (pages 78-82)

The purpose of these pages is to teach the students to recognize which people in each picture are being left out. These pages depict familiar situations in which some children are excluded from an activity or group. This visual cue will help students build awareness of the importance of *inclusion.* Each student will need a copy of the activity sheet, a blue crayon, and a yellow crayon. The teacher may ask students to identify the children being included and color them with the yellow crayon, since *yellow* is a happy color, and to find those being left out and color them with the blue crayon, since *blue* is another word for *sad.* After the students have identified and colored the children being included and those being excluded, ask why a child who is left out or excluded would be sad.

FRIENDS FIRST CERTIFICATE (page 83)

The purpose of this activity is for students to sign a *Friends First Certificate* to remind themselves to talk things out and to never gossip. Each student will need a copy of the *Certificate* and a pencil. The students may compose amendments to the *Certificate* and add names of mediators who will help if needed. During the discussion, the teacher may refer to Amendments to the *Constitution* and explain when and why they were added. This discussion may also include reviews of *conflict resolution* and *mediation techniques*.

EVERYONE IS BETTER THAN ONLY A FEW (page 84)

The purpose of this activity is to give each student an opportunity to create a collage from pictures cut out of magazines. Instruct the students to find pictures of people of different ages, skin color, gender, eye color, hair color, clothing styles, etc. Each student will need a copy of the activity sheet, magazines, a gluestick, and scissors. Display the finished collages to the class. Then mount the finished collages on different colors of construction paper and post them on the bulletin board. Discuss, with the class, the differences among individuals and the beauty in all people.

RELATIONAL AGGRESSION WORD SEARCH (page 85)

The purpose of this activity is to help students practice spelling vocabulary words by finding and circling them in the word search. Each student will need a copy of the activity sheet and a pencil.

RELATIONAL AGGRESSION CROSSWORD PUZZLE (page 86)

The purpose of this activity is to help students learn the meanings of the vocabulary words used in this program. Each student will need a copy of the activity sheet and a pencil.

R	B	X	Q	Q	V	R	G	J	Q	U	K	P	W
E	E	Y	K	K	S	U	O	P	O	G	I	N	E
X	V	L	L	A	N	W	X	M	R	S	O	I	K
C	P	I	A	A	V	J	I	Y	S	I	E	N	F
L	J	Y	F	T	W	D	B	O	S	C	Q	C	P
U	I	T	E	Z	I	C	G	S	P	X	S	L	U
D	M	H	F	O	R	O	E	E	L	Z	M	U	R
E	E	A	H	B	B	R	N	B	X	M	L	D	P
H	O	B	X	Y	G	P	R	S	V	A	Y	E	O
N	I	B	Y	G	L	A	S	R	H	I	T	K	S
P	W	U	A	I	D	W	A	N	X	I	R	G	E
H	Q	Z	T	H	R	E	A	T	E	N	P	T	L
I	N	V	I	T	A	T	I	O	N	G	O	T	Y
W	B	A	A	K	P	R	E	S	I	D	E	N	T

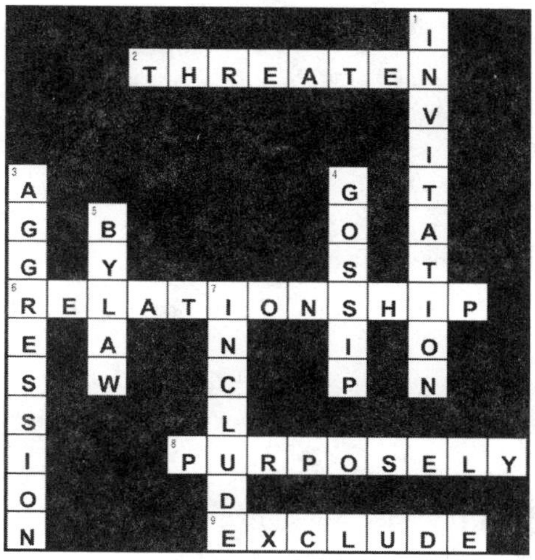

INCLUSION MOBILE

The purpose of this activity is to teach students to equate *inclusion* with happy feelings. Each student will need a camera, tagboard, rubber cement, scissors, yarn, a hole punch, a coat hanger, and a marker. The students may use the school digital camera or disposable cameras to take pictures of the faces of happy children. (If no camera is available, the students may draw happy faces.) Cut the tagboard into circles, squares, triangles, and other shapes. Use rubber cement to mount the pictures on tagboard. On the back of each mounted picture, have the students write words or phrases that are used to include people. Suggested words or phrases are: *Let's play together; Come over to my house; I like you; etc.* You may want to have the students discuss phrases like these before writing them on the backs of the pictures. Have the students cut a piece of tagboard into a rectangular shape and write on it: *Friendly words equal happy faces*. Punch a hole through the top of each picture. Cut pieces of yarn into various lengths and string a piece of yarn through the hole in the top of each picture. Tie the yarn to the coat hanger. Select two pictures and punch a hole in the bottom of each. Place these pictures close to each other and below the mounted pictures. Punch two holes in the top of the rectangular piece of tagboard. Thread yarn through the rectangular piece of tagboard and through the two pictures with holes at the bottom. The mobile will now include pictures and a title. Suspend the mobile from the ceiling.

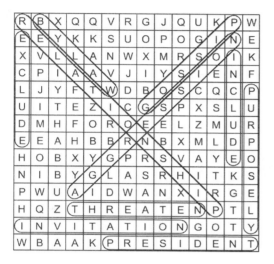

Friendly Food

Name ____

Directions: People who have come to our country have brought favorite foods from their homelands. We accepted everyone. The United States was known as a *melting pot*. Color the pictures of your favorite foods, cut them out, and paste them in the pot.

Include/Exclude

Name ______________________________

Directions: Below are two circles. One is for you to fill by writing words that *include*. The other circle is for you to fill by writing words that *exclude.* Look at the words next to the circles. Decide if each word has to do with *including* or *excluding.* Then write each word in the correct circle.

HAPPY
JOYFUL
BUSY
EXCITED
CONTENT
PLAYFUL
CHEERY
CONFUSED
UNWANTED
LONELY
HELPLESS
SAD
ANGRY
HURT

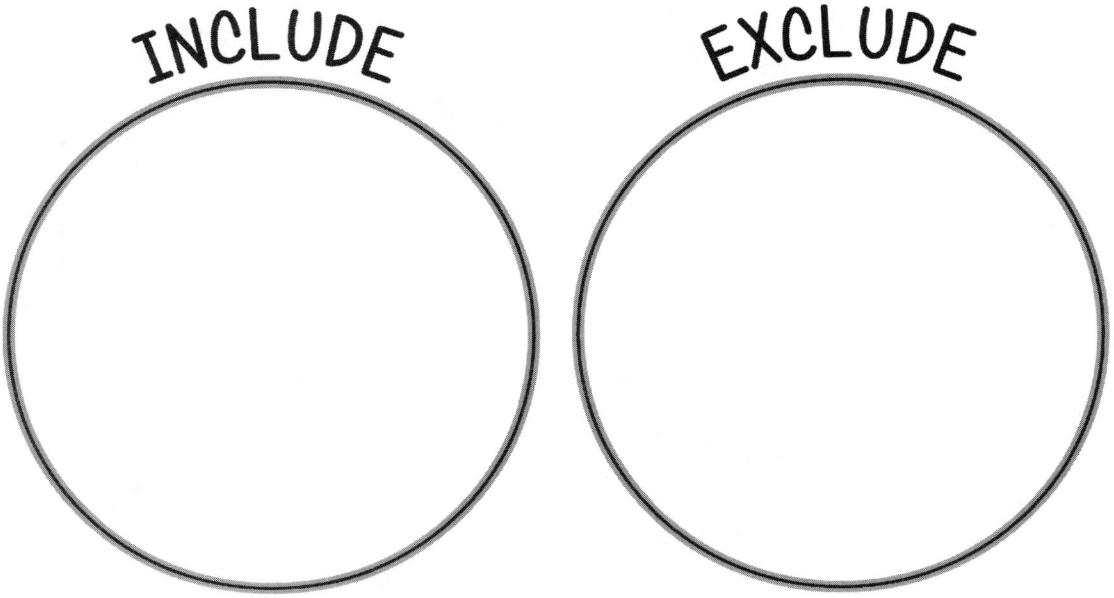

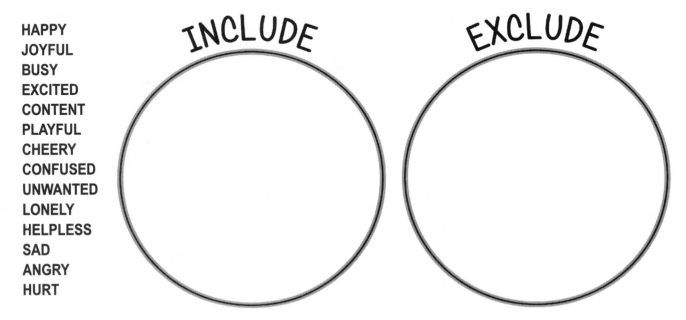

Directions: On the line following each sentence, mark *I* for words that *include* and *E* for words that *exclude.*

1. Would you like to play with me? ________
2. Only third-graders may play here. ________
3. Can you come to my house after school? ________
4. Go home! ________
5. You have to wear shoes like ours if you want to play with us. ________
6. No boys allowed! ________
7. Call me after school. ________
8. We have a club and you can't join it. ________
9. You can't play. ________
10. How about eating lunch with our group? ________
11. Will you walk with me to the library? ________

The Gossip Guarantee

Name ____

Directions: Look at the characters in each cartoon panel. They are gossiping. Write a sentence to show what the characters in the first panel are saying. In the second panel, write the sentence you wrote in the first panel, but change one word. Change one word in the sentence for each panel until you reach the end. Then compare the sentences in the first and last panels.

The Gossip Guarantee:
Every time something is repeated, it changes in some way. Sometimes the words change. Sometimes the change is in the speaker's tone of voice or intent. Ask a grown-up about *gossip*. Does it go away when you are older? Ask how to guard against gossip. Gossiping is a waste of time and hurtful.

Snowflakes

Name ____

Directions: Look at the picture of the snowflake on this activity sheet. Cut it out. If you wish, you may change the snowflake by not cutting it out exactly as it is shown. Then draw another snowflake on the paper your teacher gave you. When you have finished drawing the snowflake, cut it out and post it on the bulletin board.

Like people, snowflakes are all different. Imagine what your bulletin board would look like with only one or two snowflakes on it. It would not look as nice as it does now with lots of different snowflakes. The same thing is true about people. It is nice to include lots of people in your group of friends. When you include lots of friends, you get to enjoy many personalities. The more friends you include, the more fun you will have.

Invisible Ink Club

Name ____

Directions: Use lemon juice to make invisible ink. Then use a small paintbrush or a cotton swab to write the name of your club on the poster below. After the invisible ink has dried, have a teacher or parent rub lightly over it with a warm iron. The name of your club will appear!

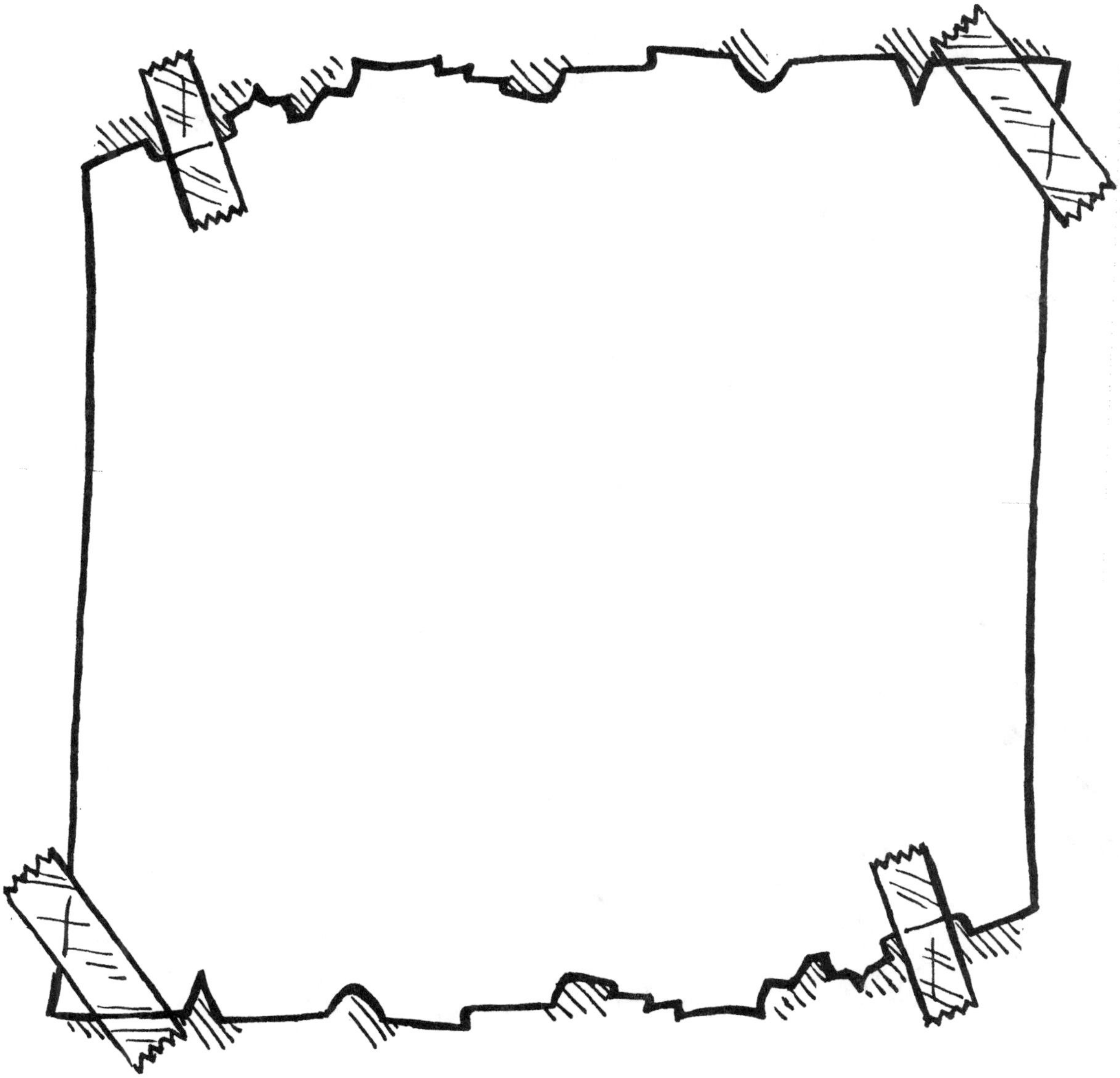

Some people have secret clubs. It's fun to pretend your club is a secret, but it's more fun to include everyone. It's important to include Mom and Dad, because they are wise and can help you make choices. Every club has a Board of Directors. Club members elect the Board of Directors to make good choices for the group. Your club's Board of Directors should include parents and teachers. They can help you be safe and have fun.

Parade

Name ____

Directions: Give an instrument to each band member who doesn't have one. Draw a line from each band member without an instrument to an instrument.

In any musical group, each instrument helps make one beautiful sound. If we leave anyone out, we are making our group weaker.

Excluding/Including Vowels

Name ____

Directions: When we talk about *excluding* something or someone, we are talking about *leaving someone or something out.* Something important has been left out of each of the words below. The VOWELS are missing! Look at the words. On the line after each word, rewrite the word and include the vowels. In the other column, list the words in alphabetical order.

WORD WITHOUT VOWELS	WORD WITH VOWELS	ALPHABETICAL ORDER
Gssp	____________	____________
rltnshp	____________	____________
ggrssn	____________	____________
prsdnt	____________	____________
blws	____________	____________
ncld	____________	____________
xcld	____________	____________
nvttn	____________	____________
thrtn	____________	____________
prpsly	____________	____________

Compare And Contrast Letter

Name ____

Directions: Write a letter to a toxic friend. Tell your friend about the times he/she has been kind to you. Then contrast that statement with examples of your friend's unkindness. Be sure to use an "I" Message to tell your friend how his/her behavior makes you feel.

Dear ______________________________,

I like playing with you on most days. I like when we

play ____________________________. Sometimes you do

things that bother me. I feel ________________________

when you ____.

Next time you think about ___________________________,

I want you to ______________________________________.

Sincerely,

____

Meet me at the

____

at recess
for a
fun game!

Save a

slice
of the day
for me!

Friendship Greetings

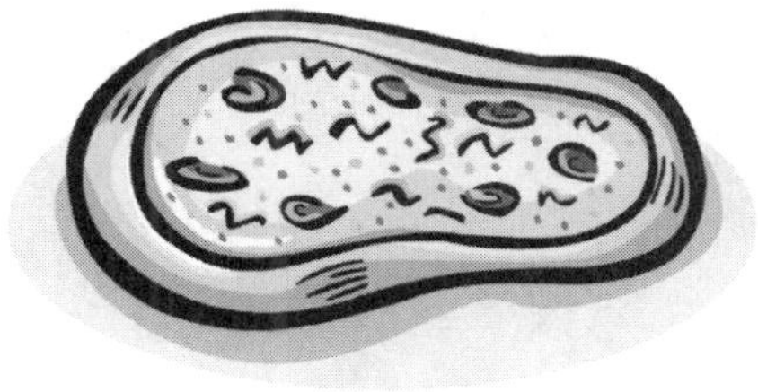

MAR*CO PRODUCTS, INC.

Meet me at the

at recess.

Bring a

Friendship Greetings

MAR*CO PRODUCTS, INC.

Let's Get Together!

Meet me at the

at recess.

Bring a

Let's Get Together!

Friendship Greetings

MAR*CO PRODUCTS, INC.

What Is Wendy's Talent?

Name ____

Directions: Connect the dots to find Wendy's talent.

Get The Bugs Into The Jar

Name ____

Directions: Follow each line to help the bugs get back into the jar.

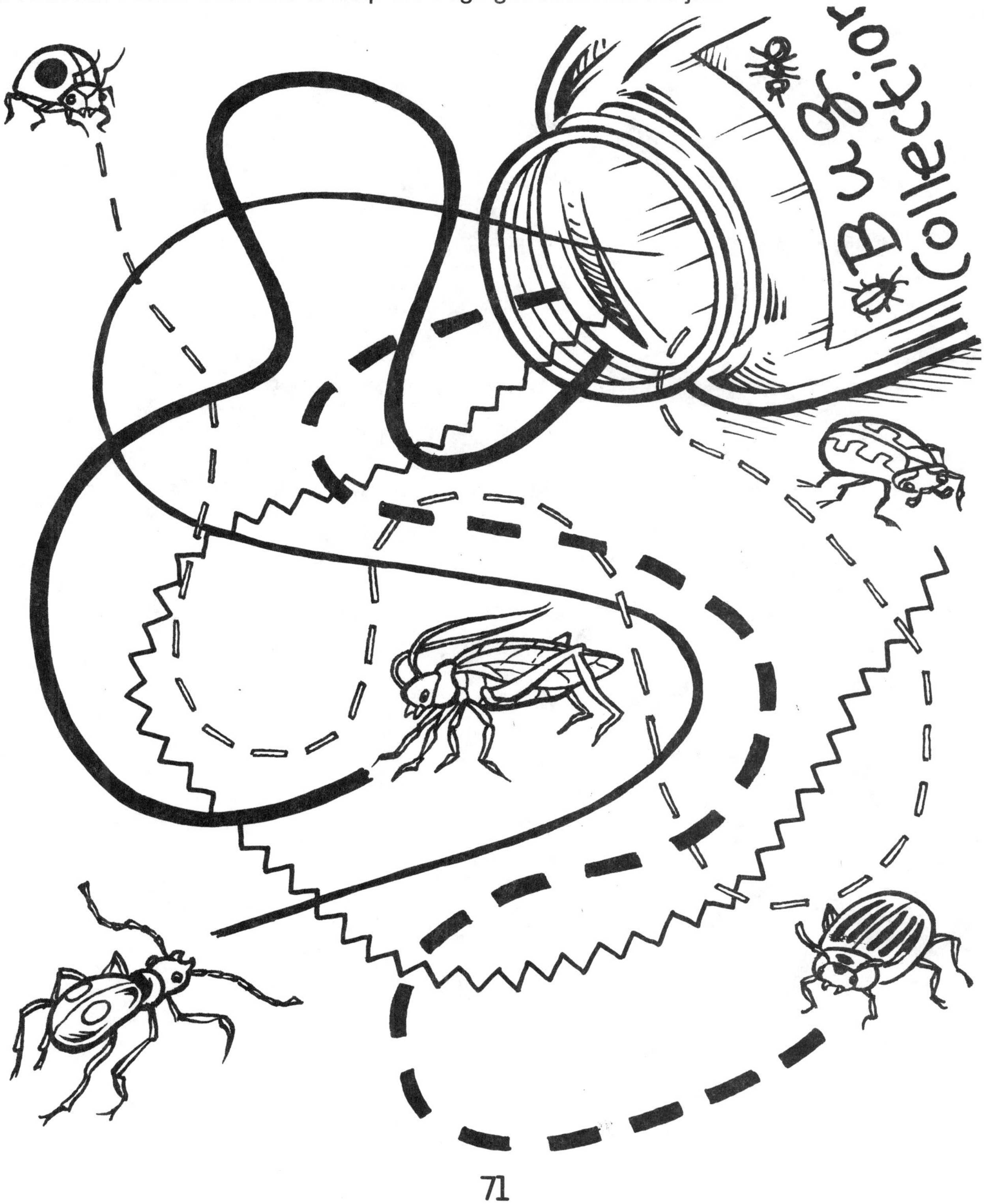

Find Wendy's Hidden Talents

Name ____

Directions: Look closely to find the hidden pictures. Wendy had many hidden talents. It was important for her sisters to look closely to find what they liked about her. When you find the pictures of Wendy's talents, color them. Be on the lookout for the good things your friends do and the talents they have.

EXs AND INs

Name ____

Directions: Use a dictionary to find words that begin with *ex* or *in*. Each word you find must be able to stand alone without *in* or *ex* (like *ex**ample*** and *in**crease***). See how long you can make your list. If you don't know the word already, turn your paper over and write the definition on the back.

EXs	INs
______________________	______________________
______________________	______________________
______________________	______________________
______________________	______________________
______________________	______________________
______________________	______________________
______________________	______________________
______________________	______________________
______________________	______________________
______________________	______________________
______________________	______________________
______________________	______________________
______________________	______________________
______________________	______________________

Bug Friends

Name ____

Directions: Look closely at the bugs and circle those that are exactly alike. Do we have to have friends who are just like us?

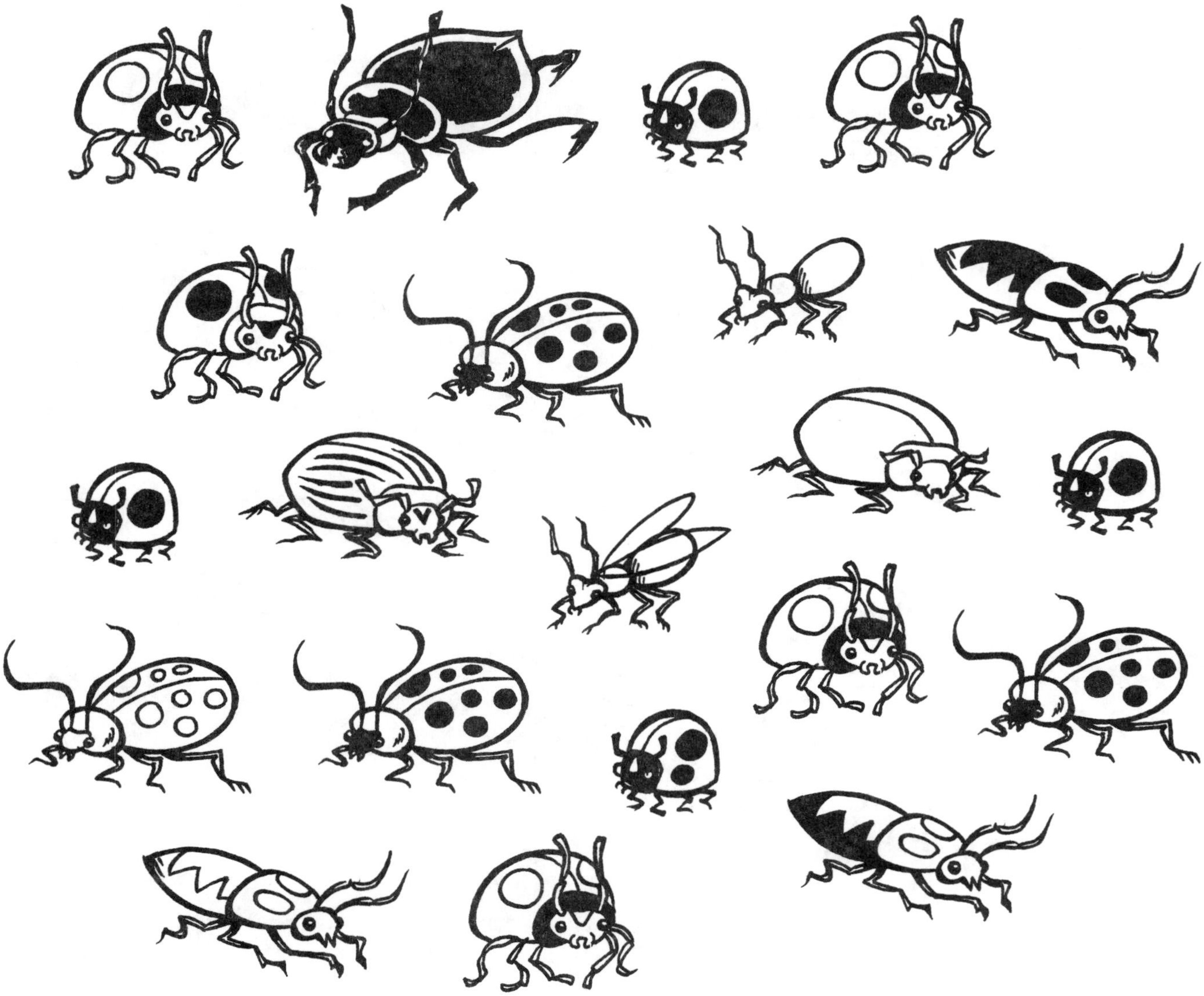

My Secret Club Message

Name ____

Directions: Match the letters to the numbers and write a secret message for your club. Put a line above each number and a space after each word.

24	a	15	j	6	s
23	b	14	k	5	t
22	c	13	l	4	u
21	d	12	m	3	v
20	e	11	n	2	w
19	f	10	o	1	x
18	g	9	p	26	y
17	h	8	q	25	z
16	i	7	r		

Secret messages are fun!

Make sure everyone is in on the fun. Give your code to all of your friends and write to them after school. Remember not to pass notes in class.

How Many Words Can You Make?

Name ____

Directions: How many words can you make from the letters in *Relational Aggression?* You may use only the letters in these words to form other words. There are three a's in *Relational Aggression,* for example. So your new word may include 1, 2, or 3 a's, but not more.

RELATIONAL AGGRESSION

_________________________ _________________________

_________________________ _________________________

_________________________ _________________________

_________________________ _________________________

_________________________ _________________________

_________________________ _________________________

_________________________ _________________________

_________________________ _________________________

_________________________ _________________________

Make A Case For Your Friend

Name ____

Directions: It is easy to find the faults of people who are mean to us. But everyone has good qualities. On the first of the cases below, list the things your friend is doing that are bothering you. On the second case, list the things you like about your friend. Then write an answer to the question below.

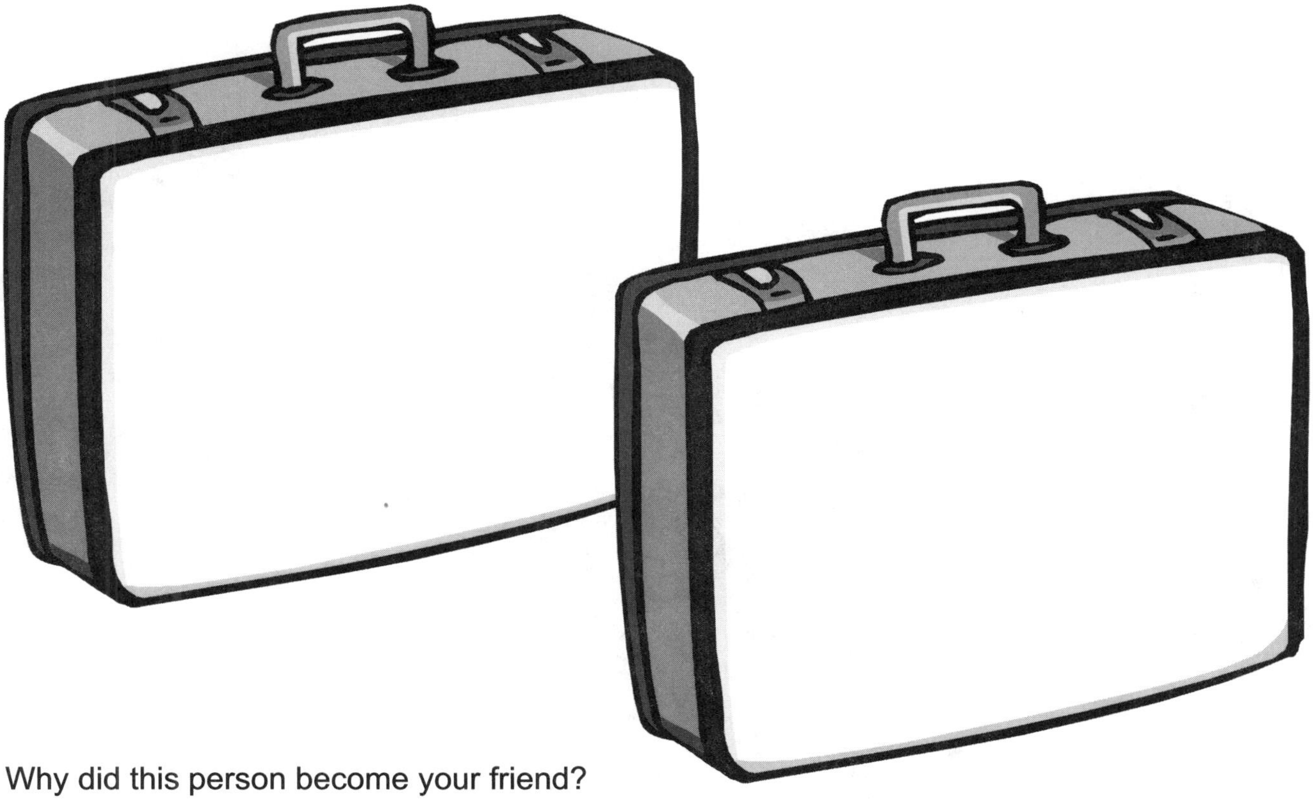

Why did this person become your friend?

____

____

____

Sometimes just remembering the good things about a friend can get you over a bad spot. If that doesn't work, talk with your friend about how you feel when he/she is unkind to you. Use the list to give examples of your friend's behavior so he/she will know what to do to be a better friend. Be ready to listen to your friend's ideas. You might be causing problems, too.

Everyone Doesn't Love A Parade

Name ____

Directions: Find the person or persons being left out. Use your blue crayon to color the person or persons being excluded. Use your yellow crayon to color the persons being included.

Lunchtime Isn't Fun For Everyone

Name ____

Directions: Find the person or persons being left out. Use your blue crayon to color the person or persons being excluded. Use your yellow crayon to color the persons being included.

Not Everyone Gets To Play

Name ____

Directions: Find the person or persons being left out. Use your blue crayon to color the person or persons being excluded. Use your yellow crayon to color the persons being included.

Why Wasn't I Invited To The Party?

Name ____

Directions: Find the person or persons being left out. Use your blue crayon to color the person or persons being excluded. Use your yellow crayon to color the persons being included.

Private Club

Name ____

Directions: Find the person or persons being left out. Use your blue crayon to color the person or persons being excluded. Use your yellow crayon to color the persons being included.

Friends First Certificate

We, the undersigned, agree that if we have a problem with a friend, we'll talk things out as friends and not gossip to others about the problem.

____

____

____

____

Everyone Is Better Than Only A Few

Name ____

Directions: Make a collage with people cut out of magazines. Include as many different types of people as you can find. Don't leave anyone out.

Relational Aggression Word Search

Name ____

Directions: Find the words below in the word search. When you find each word, circle it. Words may be spelled from side to side, on a slant, from top to bottom, or from bottom to top.

GOSSIP	RELATIONSHIP	AGGRESSION
PRESIDENT	BYLAW	INCLUDE
EXCLUDE	INVITATION	THREATEN
PURPOSELY		

R	B	X	Q	Q	V	R	G	J	Q	U	K	P	W
E	E	Y	K	K	S	U	O	P	O	G	I	N	E
X	V	L	L	A	N	W	X	M	R	S	O	I	K
C	P	I	A	A	V	J	I	Y	S	I	E	N	F
L	J	Y	F	T	W	D	B	O	S	C	Q	C	P
U	I	T	E	Z	I	C	G	S	P	X	S	L	U
D	M	H	F	O	R	O	E	E	L	Z	M	U	R
E	E	A	H	B	B	R	N	B	X	M	L	D	P
H	O	B	X	Y	G	P	R	S	V	A	Y	E	O
N	I	B	Y	G	L	A	S	R	H	I	T	K	S
P	W	U	A	I	D	W	A	N	X	I	R	G	E
H	Q	Z	T	H	R	E	A	T	E	N	P	T	L
I	N	V	I	T	A	T	I	O	N	G	O	T	Y
W	B	A	A	K	P	R	E	S	I	D	E	N	T

Relational Aggression Crossword Puzzle

Name ____

Directions: Complete the crossword puzzle below.

ACROSS
2. to indicate a plan to do something mean
6. a feeling that exists between people
8. deliberately
9. shut out or reject

DOWN
1. note or message used to ask someone to do something or go somewhere
3. an attack, assault, or hostile behavior
4. to repeat something someone has told you or to talk about someone's private business
5. rule or law of a club
7. let in or contain

DEBRA WOSNIK

Debra Wosnik graduated from California Polytechnic University with a bachelor's degree in behavioral science. She received her teaching credential from Fresno State University and her master's in education/counseling from the University of Phoenix. She has taught elementary school in California and Utah and was coordinator of programs for gifted students in two districts in the San Joaquin Valley. She is currently an elementary counselor.

Debra is the mother of five children and the wife of an elementary principal. But best of all, she is a grandma who is really good at reading stories! Her story *Fair Is Where Grandma Took Her Pickles In The Fall* (from *Life Isn't Always Fair*) tells of her life with four sisters. The girls in the story are now adults, and they all have different talents. Cherie is a college professor. Wendy is a therapist. Mary Anne is a French teacher and artist, and Holly is a mom.